LADIHOOD

There is an Art to Being a Lady

The Lady's "Pursebook" of Gentle Reminders

Monique Stubbs-Hall

Copyright © 2015 by Monique Stubbs-Hall

Published by Monique Stubbs-Hall

All Rights Reserved.

No part of this book may be reproduced, stored in a retrieval system, or transmitted by any means without the written permission of the publisher. The scanning, uploading and distribution of this book via the internet without the written permission of the publisher is prohibited. Your support of the author's rights is appreciated.

Visit www.MoniqueTalks.com to contact the author.

Printing History
Edition One, August 2015

ISBN-13: 978-0692523636

This book is dedicated to the Ladies who mean the most to me in my life:

It all begins with:

My Mother Stephanie M. Stubbs
The Epitome of a Lady

Thank you Mom for instilling in me all of the wonderful qualities that allow me to stand out as you do, as a woman of dignity and grace

My Sister Cristal O. Moncur

Thank you Cristal for joining me in passing on the legacy of our Mother to your two young ladies, my Nieces Morgan and Sydney

My Beautiful Daughters
Monet, Chloe and Victoria

Mommy hopes that you will be inspired to continue applying what I have passed on to you in all that you do. Never be ashamed to conduct yourself as a lady and realize that grace, dignity, strength and character will cause you to stand out from the crowd and will result in admiration and respect from those that observe you. I love you all and pray that as you mature into beautiful young ladies you will pass these values on to the next generation.

A girl should be two things

Classy & Fabulous

—Coco Chanel

The Contents of Your "Pursebook"

Love yourself enough to make necessary changes

Reminder 1

Arrogance will hinder your growth

Reminder 2

Dare to be Dainty

Reminder 3

Ignorance is not cute

Reminder 4

Hide your thighs from our eyes

Reminder 5

Overdone is out of style

Reminder 6

Open your eyes to see the real you

Reminder 7

Don't allow anyone to undermine you or your talent

Reminder 8

LADIHOOD

The Lady's "Pursebook" of Gentle Reminders

Gentle Reminder 1

Love Yourself Enough To Make Necessary Changes

Change is not easy for any of us. You must realize that a true lady realizes that change at times is necessary. Change helps to build your character. Making changes requires humility and for many this quality is difficult to master. When areas of improvement are brought to your attention by those you admire and respect, realize it is for your betterment. Instead of fighting them, take what they have shared to heart and make the necessary adjustments. Staying stuck and stubborn is not becoming. This could be a clear indication that you have not cultivated a love great enough for yourself to make necessary changes.

I'm committed to making the following improvements in this area:

_____
_____
_____
_____
_____
_____
_____
_____
_____
_____

Beautiful

✔️ *A Check Point from Grandma on sitting like a Lady*

"Never sit with your legs wide open, honey-you don't want the whole world to see your business"

Gentle Reminder 2

Arrogance Will Hinder Your Growth

Remember there is nothing worse than an arrogant woman. Arrogance is far from ladylike. Strive to demonstrate **confidence** not arrogance. What is the difference?

An **arrogant** individual only feels smart when someone else feels stupid. How do you identify them? They are constantly putting other's down, they take pride in talking about themselves excessively and they tend to attract friends who hang with them when times are good and roll out when times are bad.

A **confident** individual feels competent from the inside out. They use their talents to try to be of use to others. While they are confident, they are humble and attract friends who are loyal. They obtain lasting relationships and long term success and a better quality of life.

So make it a goal not to stunt your growth into "Ladihood" by having an arrogant attitude. A lady who is quietly confident in her abilities takes an interest in the welfare and feelings of others, and as a result, prospers.

I'm committed to making the following improvements in this area:

_____
_____
_____
_____
_____
_____
_____
_____
_____
_____

Confident

✔ *A Check Point from Grandma on having a bad attitude!*

"Roll your eyes one more time and I'm gonna take them out!"

Gentle Reminder 3

Dare to Be Dainty

Dainty is always in! …..Raunchy (or as Grandma would say "uncouth") is out! Since when is it acceptable as a female to act "rough around the edges"? There is nothing wrong with crossing your legs or tucking them to your side when sitting down. Walking with grace and proper posture is important hold your head up and straighten your back. Allow gentlemen to open the car door for you and wait for them to pull the chair out for you. If you carry yourself as a lady, these niceties will even come your way without requesting it. Take the time to learn how to eat properly with a fork and knife. Learn in a formal setting the appropriate silverware to selections as you move through the courses of a meal. Remember that a "please" and "thank you" go a long way. Choose the course of daintiness and dare to stand out from the rest!

I'm committed to making the following improvements in this area:

_____
_____
_____
_____
_____
_____
_____
_____
_____
_____

Enthusiastic

A Check Point from Grandma on manners at the dining table

"Belchin', pickin' your teeth and passin' gas at the table just ain't lady like, hone...please excuse yourself and take that somewhere else!"

Gentle Reminder 4

Ignorance Is Not Cute

The statement above is so bold that it stands on its own without further explanation. However at this point, all that I can provide are examples of ignorant behavior that a Lady will refuse to engage in:

STOP **rolling YOUR eyes.** This has to be one of the most annoying and disrespectful gestures you can make! There is nothing else to be said other than DON'T DO IT!

STOP **making a scene in public when you can't have your way.** Learn self-control and stop acting like a spoiled brat! Show with intelligent speech that you can express your disapproval of a situation without having to throw a public temper tantrum.

STOP **smacking and clicking gum while someone is speaking to you.** Aside from not being lady like…Grandma would say "you look like a cow chewing on its cud" it's just plain unattractive.

STOP **using verbal and visual profanities.** Cursing and calling people names and using inappropriate gestures with your fingers is unacceptable and shows your own weakness of not being able to communicate in acceptable words.

STOP **staring people down because as you say "they think they are cute".** Most likely they are…get over it!

I'm committed to making the following improvements in this area:

_____
_____
_____
_____
_____
_____
_____
_____
_____

Brilliant

✔️ *A Check Point from Grandma on your clothing choice*

"Are you sure that's what you are wearin' out the house today? Hmmm…you look a HOT MESS!"

Gentle Reminder 5

Hide Your Thighs From Our Eyes

From the day I heard this expression I thought it was the perfect reminder on modesty. Of course the expression above has to do with skirt lengths. It is a ladies reminder that if your thighs are showing your skirt is just too short. Remember, if your thighs are hanging out while you are standing up, when you sit down other things may be exposed as well. So always be mindful of those skirt lengths.

It is true that we all have a choice of what we want to wear. However, it is important that as a lady you understand that not all fashions are fashionable. Not all fashions are appropriate for your size. Realize that there is a time and a place for certain fashions. For example, wearing "night club" attire to your job would be inappropriate. Therefore, you will always be safe if you remember the following: "be modest", know when to wear what type of attire" and "if it doesn't fit, it doesn't fit!".

I'm committed to making the following improvements in this area:

_____
_____
_____
_____
_____
_____
_____
_____
_____
_____
_____

Wise

✓ *A Check Point from Grandma on modesty*

"Sweetheart…when you are trying to decide on whether to buy an outfit try this :

1. Stand in front of a mirror with a light shining behind you.

2. Spread your legs!

3. If you can see thru it you need a slip or another choice!

4. Bend forward, look in the mirror, if you can see your chest or between them the outfit is too low!

5. Turn around and look at your backside, can you see dimples and layers…it's too tight!

6. Take it off and try something else…`cause it's just not goin' to work!"

Gentle Reminder 6

Overdone is Out of Style

How many times have we heard the expression, "too much of anything is not good?" Well this can apply in women's efforts to be a lady. We see a lot of "Overdone" in our society which takes certain aspects of being a lady over the edge.

Too much makeup can give the impression that you look like a clown, rather than a lady. If in doubt, consult a professional in that area. Too much jewelry is a distraction, so keep the number of holes and earrings running up your ears to a tasteful amount. A ring on every finger is not necessary. If you must wear multiple rings, fashion consultants say select one finger on each hand, but that's it.

Body piercing and tattoos are all touchy subjects. If you feel you must have them make sure that you don't overdo it. It is important that they can be covered up for times where exposing them is inappropriate. So if you desire to pass an interview and/or get hired in a professional environment, you will want to give attention to where you choose to pierce or tattoo your body. Stay away from piercings and tattoos up your neck, on your face, below a short sleeved shirt line and below a shorts line on your legs.

Hairstyles have also gone out of control! Watch faddish hairstyles and make sure that the style you wear is appropriate for the environment you work in. Watch your choice of hair colors. Florescent fuchsia, yellow and green hair colors, may be appropriate for Halloween or some specific event, but not on a daily basis. When in doubt, do without!

I'm committed to making the following improvements in this area:

_____

_____

_____

_____

_____

_____

_____

_____

_____

_____

Caring

✓ *A Check Point from Grandma On Domestic Violence*

"Don't ever let a man put his hands on you…if he tries to, 'a pot of hot grits' always works!"

Gentle Reminder 7

Open Your Eyes To See The Real You

Sometimes we can be caught up in following others so much so that we lose sight of who we are. Peer pressure is real whether you are young or old. Be cautious of who you choose to be in your circle of friends. Wrong choices can result in you being around people who negatively influence you. People who do not have your best interest at heart will make decisions based upon their own agenda, which may not always in set with your values. Look around and ask yourself: are they inspiring me to be the good person I want to be or are they always trying to force me to be something that I am not ? If the answer is the latter, it's time to Open Your Eyes, find a more positive circle of influence and work on reaching your fullest potential. A lady who can look in the mirror and identify her true self and talents and be comfortable with them is on the road to great endeavors!

I'm committed to making the following improvements in this area:

_____
_____
_____
_____
_____
_____
_____
_____
_____
_____

Creative

✓ *A Check Point from Grandma Chastity!*

"Just because you think you are so cute that you can catch every Tom, Dick and Harry-remember sweetheart you can get caught with the diseases that every one of them carries!
Save yourself for that special one…plus remember, if you pop up pregnant I'm too old to be raisin' a baby… so you are on your own with that one!"

Gentle Reminder 8

Don't Allow Anyone to Undermine You or Your Talents

Now we could discuss this topic forever because I am very passionate about this. There is no one on the face of this earth that is worth having around in your life if they cannot respect you. Anyone who chooses to verbally, physically or mentally abuse you is not worthy of your time or space. RUN FROM THEM!!!! Those who are abusive behave this way because of their own insecurities and inadequacies. They want to feel superior to you and so they do this by treating you as though you are inferior. DON'T FEED INTO IT! Your stand should be NON-NEGOTIABLE! If you are in this type of a relationship and you feel you need help please seek help from someone you trust or the help of professionals. If your life is at risk please bring in the law if necessary. You are a lady and not a punching bag, you are a delicate flower that should be cherished and not demolished, you have inborn talents that the world needs to see so don't allow anyone to abuse you!

I'm committed to making the following improvements in this area:

_____
_____
_____
_____
_____
_____
_____
_____
_____
_____
_____
_____

Captivating

Place your 8 Gentle Reminders in your purse to keep them close to you at all times. Feel free to share them with anyone who you feel may benefit. May we pass these reminders on to generations to come, so that the values of "Ladihood" are never lost.

LADIHOOD the Acronym

L *ove yourself enough to make necessary changes*
A *rrogance will hinder your growth*
D *are to be dainty*
I *gnorance is not cute*
H *ide your thighs from our eyes*
O *verdone is out of style*
O *pen your eyes to see the real you*
D *on't allow anyone to undermine you or your talents*

Successful

Where It All Began

Many wonder why the term Ladihood? Since I have a passion for the grooming of our young girls into ladies, I also realize that "it takes a village" to raise them. Our youth are not equipped to decipher the explicit and <u>negative</u> messages about women that television, radio and other forms of media expose them to on a daily basis.

The expression "hood" has become a term that reflects poverty in society. However, I choose to view it as simply a term that reflects a community. So we are creating a "hood" or "community" of ladies and changing the perception of that term. The "Ladihood Movement" will grow internationally as more and more in the community recognize the need for guardians to bond with their young girls through the grooming process.

It is our desire that you utilize this "Pursebook" of gentle reminders as a mother, guardian or mentor with your girls to facilitate open discussions regarding their grooming. By strengthening your bond with your young lady, we hope to build stronger family ties and in so doing, you can help enrich your "hood" or "community".

Please enjoy the poetic piece that is the inspiration behind the "Ladihood Movement"!

LADIHOOD

Ladihood
If it's not a word yet,
I'm creating it.

Hope you don't object,
But I'm addressing it.

Ladihood
Definition: The Art of Being A Lady.

Or maybe it's not yet been defined because it's lacking
Because, Mother's today in teaching it are slacking.

Where are the ladies today?
Where are the role models that can show them the way to
Ladihood?

Our little girls are truly lacking,
No fault of their own, mommas leave so early in the morning

With a peck on the cheek and a pat on the back
We send our babies out there and pray they will stay on track

But reality is sobering indeed
There are so few women out there to take the lead

To teach them "Ladihood".

Will we leave it to the so-called role models today,
Everything skin tight and hangin' out is their way!

With foul mouths, suggestive moves and exploitations beyond belief,
Through video and t.v. that have become the thief.

To snatch away finesse,
And groom our little girls into a "hot mess"!

Gone are the days of gloves and gowns
Of hats and couture that would spin heads around

Back in our mamma and grand mamma's day
Ladihood was the only way!

Where are the ladies whose style and grace seemed inborn?
Women such as Katherine Hepburn and Lena Horne

Consider women whose dignity and strength would ring,
We have bold women such as Coretta Scott-King.

And yes we have examples of classy mammas,
Like Princess Dianna and Michelle Obama!

So mammas I'm asking you to check where you've stood?
Are you grooming your little girls into "Ladihood"?

Copyright by: Monique Stubbs-Hall
October 31, 2011

Stay Beautiful ♡

ABOUT MONIQUE STUBBS-HALL

Founder of LADIHOOD

Monique Stubbs-Hall is a Native of Nassau, Bahamas and now a resident of Charlotte, NC. She has an extensive background in both Cosmetic and Hospitality Sales and Public Speaking with over 20yrs experience in both. She is married and a Mother of 4 children. Monique has a passion for serving others! She loves to encourage others to not just achieve external beauty but to cultivate the qualities that build inner beauty. She strongly believes that a parent's good example in mentoring, demonstrating a strong work ethic and cultivating good communication with their children sets a strong stage for their growth and success in life. Monique is an Entrepreneur, Inspirational Speaker, Author and Poet. Her first published work is entitled "Love Ain't Pain Free (2006) written as a journey of self-discovery. She is excited about her newest written work entitled "Ladihood - The Art of Being a Lady" which embodies her desire to empower parents to groom their young girls into "Ladies". As she always says "Dainty is never out of style"!

Her unique quality is the ability to captivate any type of audience from large corporate events to small intimate settings. She is known for her versatility. She can easily move from a classic suit environment for workshops and discourses into gown and gloves for an elegant evening of poetry (she is affectionately called the "Billie Holliday of Poetry"). Her professional yet enthusiastic personality is intriguing. Monique's favorite quote is "Despite life's ups and downs, you must take time to enjoy life's journey".

Visit www.MoniqueTalks.com to:

~ Subscribe
~ Learn more about her upcoming events and workshops
~ Order other publications
~ Book Monique for speaking engagements

LADIHOOD

www.ingramcontent.com/pod-product-compliance
Lightning Source LLC
Chambersburg PA
CBHW041526090426
42736CB00035B/32